Nowheresville, Everywhere, Earth

by

Donna Lee

authorHOUSE®

AuthorHouse™
1663 Liberty Drive, Suite 200
Bloomington, IN 47403
www.authorhouse.com
Phone: 1-800-839-8640

First published by AuthorHouse 5/1/2008

ISBN: 978-1-4343-5869-1 (sc)

Printed in the United States of America
Bloomington, Indiana

This book is printed on acid-free paper.

"My Informed Opinions on Higher Education" was the first piece
published on www.thenoyse.com in its Editorials Section in 4/05 and
www.ithinkthereforeimdangerous.g2gm.com

"My and Five Others' Views on the Primary Purposes of Education"
published Winter 2006 issue of Education Revolution magazine/www.
educationrevolution.org

Cover design: Donna Lee & Julio Jimenez/GTC
Media/www.clubflyers.com

To all those who love learning, truth, and me!

Contents

Nowheresville, Everywhere, Earth

Is THERE A place for me anywhere in your hearts? That is my eternal question. It comes from my razor's edge walk between life and death, producing the tertium non datur, or the unknown third, which incorporates and transcends the two: rebirth, also known as redemption, known, too, as power. Not the love of power, but the power of love.

I have been studying the psychological theories of Carl Jung, also known as Analytical Psychology, meant to be a synthesis of all systems of such thought, as a layperson/autodidact for the past 25 years. I've come across many analysts, in their practices and through their written works, including many of Jung's works. In all that time, I have never met a black one!

This dawned on me forcefully in June as I was descending a hill (as I am in the descent of my life) and I met a young black woman ascending the hill (as she is doing in her life) who had an elaborately coiffed hairstyle, yet was dressed in the most ordinary jeans, t-shirt, and sneakers. I couldn't resist stopping her as our paths crossed to get a closer look and to comment on this odd sight.

She explained to me when I complimented her on her "do" and the contrast between it and her attire, that she had just gotten her hair done up that way for her high school prom, which was to take place that night. I then asked her if she was planning to attend college, to which she replied, "Yes," and then told me which one she was planning to attend. I then asked her what her planned major is and she said, "psychiatry." I then asked her if she'd heard of Jung to which she replied, "Yes," very firmly and confidently, immediately. Something in her manner, in spite of the brevity of her response, spoke volumes to me. It also brought the realization home to me, which I voiced above, that in all my 25 years of study, I'd never even heard of, much less met, a black analytical psychologist! Not one! This suddenly seemed strange to me. For, the very essence of analytical psychology, the process of Individuation, is about "light comprehending the darkness," so to speak. We are not only to go through this process metaphorically in our minds, but to live it in our lives and relationships.

One such, "Jim Whitney, who spoke at the Friends Conference, the year before his death," put forth the attempt at elaborating on the blending of the literal aspect of this process as well as the metaphorical aspect in the topic of his talk, which "concerned the civil-rights movement of the 1960's seen as a metaphor for the problem of integrating the light and dark sides of the psyche."[1]

As a symbol, of the best that black people have to offer, who is an almost total outsider, relegated to the dungeon of the collective American psyche, where both whites and blacks of all stripes, from professionals, to laypeople, to

[1] Janet O. Dallett, *The Not-Yet-Transformed-God Depth Psychology and the Individual Religious Experience* (York Beach: Nicolas Hayes, 1998), 99.

celebrities, to obscure "nobodies," "don't have time to," are afraid to, or simply don't want to face what I represent, as a black woman, as the embodiment of raw virgin/goddess energy, I am the perfect one to bring these dynamics to life at this time, and in this way. My studies and my struggles, though outside of, while paradoxically dead in the center of, this national conflict, have prepared me superbly for that role.

I offer, therefore, the following essays to try to bridge the yawning gap between light and dark in our psyches, hence, in our world. I think it is time. Don't you?

Dissecting Black and White Psychologically 4/11/04

The last time I was at the library, while looking for something else, I came across two thick volumes called, Visions I and Visions II, by C. G. Jung. These books are notes of the seminars Jung gave between 1930 and 1934 about visions of a female patient of his who has the same psychological type, according to Jung's typology, as I have, namely: thinking-intuitive. C. G. Jung was a Swiss psychiatrist (1875-1961), who, along with the more familiar Freud, with whom Jung associated for some years, is considered one of the founders of modern psychology.

Because I am black (African-American), and a woman (doubly dark by association in Christendom), many parts in the above mentioned writings, and in life, which pertain to "darkness" and/or "blackness," as opposed to "light" and/or "whiteness," particularly exercise my mind.

In the Western Hemisphere, where those with most of the power are white males, we all tend to see what is white or light as having the most good, being the most beneficial, and all other adjectives that suggest virtue. Even black or dark folk in the West feel this way, even if only unconsciously. On the other hand, in the unconsious at least, all Westerners equate blackness or darkness with the opposites of the above qualities yielding evil, bad, detrimental, deleterious, and destructive effects.

The Christian ethos' splitting of above from below, matter from spirit, and earth from heaven accentuated this polarity. For, in nature, we see that these extreme opposites (as is the case with all opposites or polarities) partake of one another, are the two opposing poles of a single unity, and can NEVER be fully separated one from the other for long because of those very facts. Further, no opposite by itself is completely evil and destructive, nor good and creative.

An example of this latter fact is that whole grains, or grains with their bran part intact, e.g., wheat, oats, and, rice, all brown (dark) in color, are, by far, more nutritious and healthy, and, in the long run, tasty, than highly refined foods which are very popular in the West like white (wheat, with the bran removed) flour, used to make most pasta and white bread, and white (with the bran removed) rice. The latter, especially brown rice, and rice bran, some ancient cultures, like India, have even used for medicinal purposes in the treatment of diabetes and other ills.

This is because the body metabolizes (breaks down and uses) the complex sugars in brown rice and other whole grains much more slowly than it does the highly processed and refined products, which latter contain simple sugars, the chemical bonds of which metabolize to glucose in the body almost immediately and give a rush of sugar to the cells, causing a complementary rush of insulin to process it and causing an imbalance in the system leading to diseases. Whereas, the complex sugars break down much more slowly causing less of an unbalanced and excessive insulin rush to meet them.

The processing and refinement of whole brown (dark) grains into the white food products "denatures" and destroys their balanced healthful properties and effects, as does too much conscious refinement (light, whiteness) of the human ego destroy the life-giving connection with the darker products of the unconscious. These darker, or what we consider evil contents of the human character, Jung has called, "the shadow." Just like the rice and other grain, without acknowledging as our own and assimilating our darker parts, we are not whole beings.

Everyone has a shadow, because wherever there is light cast on an object, such as the focussed illumination of consciousness in the psyche, the object casts a shadow. This is a totally natural phenomenon, which Jung discovered exists in the inner world of the psyche as well as in the outer world of physical objects.

One of the most interesting tendencies that humans have is that we project onto others these very same traits, that we don't know we possess, or that we don't wish to possess. Therefore, we see the beloved in another, when it is really our own best selves that we see but which we may not be able to acknowledge in ourselves. Or, more commonly, we see our archenemy, "the other" who is our diabolical inner twin, projected outward. The less conscious we are of the totality of our psyches, bringing more of our unconscious traits to consciousness, the stronger and more intense are our projections. Usually, when we project these qualities onto others, we are not aware that we are doing so, nor do we feel at all that the qualities we see in the other, are qualities that reside in ourselves.

The foregoing explanation of projection brings me to one of racism against people of darker color by white people, the world over. Naturally, it follows that dark skinned people are, by the very fact of their dark skin, perfect psychological "hooks" for white people to project all that is darker, that they reject, within their own psyches. Thus, all the sexual potency that the puritanical Christian white cannot admit in his own make up; his brutal, ruthless, narrowly egotistical exploitation of all the darker more self-contained peoples of the world who live more closely and in accord with the majestic, awesome even, renewing powers of the natural world, and hence the unconscious, the matrix of all life; his more primitive (or "first, primary") condition just one step above the animals and the childhood of the human species, an integral part of Nature, weak in the face of Her splendour and horror, rather than in control of Her (which no ego, black or white, wants to admit that s/he is not in control or must return to the dependent, weak, childish condition, the hazards of which, s/he just barely, and all too recently, escaped alive), the white man projects onto those, his darker brothers and sisters.

In turn, the darker peoples project their own unconscious (undeveloped) egos and lust for power and rapine and pillage, sheer domination, and perversity, of which they are not aware, but which they will acutely perpetrate against any of their own kind who is too individual, differentiated consciously, or just different in some other significant way, through shunning, debasing economically, as well as socially, her/him, as though altogether the group were a single living organism filled with cells, each of which must function the same way,

7

instead of individuals, and when one doesn't, isolating it, cutting off its nourishment, and finally expelling it to die, so that the collectivity of undifferentiated "individual" cells can live as before in the stasis which, unbeknownst to them, will eventually lead to their deaths, although something new will always be reborn from such destruction.

As Sheldon Kopp stated in his book, *If You Meet the Buddha on the Road, Kill Him!*, "All evil is energy in need of transformation." Evil is not solely inside our enemies, nor solely "out there," but resides in each and all of us. This is one of the hardest lessons for humans to learn; perhaps because it is so complex and so far away from our conscious personalities.

To integrate the shadow, or the black with the white, is an "Opus Dei," or "work of god/dess" that we must perform daily in the secret recesses of our own hearts, as well as in relationship, especially with those we "hate" the most. For this coming to wholeness, as hellishly difficult as it is, seems to be the best way (the only way, perhaps) for us to keep from using the awesome power we possess to annihilate ourselves and all of nature, thousands of times over.

In Response to a Survey Regarding Race in Essence Magazine

I DID NOT know how to answer some of your questions. That often happens when I answer surveys. However, I answered all your questions. One question that particularly stumped me was whether or not I make disparaging remarks about other races. I wasn't sure whether this also applied to other groups, as well, like religious groups, such as Jews and Chrisitans.

I cannot feel that racism among whites and their institutions, nor prejudice among blacks and theirs, will ever disappear. One very poignant reminder for me of the endurance of such negative and destructive characteristics of human nature is a statement Sheldon Kopp made in one of his books. Sheldon Kopp is a psychologist. The book of his to which I refer is, *If You Meet the Buddha on the Road, Kill Him!* This title is so ironic because one will never meet the Buddha on the road or everyone and everything one meets on the road is the Buddha.

To paraphrase Mr. Kopp, he would fight vehemently, ardently, absolutely passionately against slavery, on principle and as a social reality. However, he must admit that in fantasy, he would love to have someone to order around with impunity, whose will he could subvert, and whom he could degrade at will. He feels that the fact that he can admit this to himself (and to others) would keep him from acting upon this fantasy.

I wonder, but I think that he is right. If there is any hope for us to keep such urges in abeyance, then admitting them and bringing them out into the open is the only one. What he is admitting is, of course, a great and grievous evil.   Again, however, in his wisdom, however human and faulty, he states, and I think, rightly, that "all evil is potential vitality in need of transformation." He further states that "evil can be displaced but never eradicated, as all solutions breed new problems, yet it is necessary to keep on struggling for solution." This is what is known as a psychological perspective.

I believe this is as valid a perspective as any. It is probably even more valid than many. To transform this grievous natural human evil (not particular to any "race" more than any other), the desire to lord it over others and degrade them for one's own upliftment, is one of the hardest things for us to do. Such transformation requires change on the most fundamental of levels. Most people resist change even on the most superficial levels. The above are psychological truths which most people would do anything, and everything, except realize them. Most people especially do not want to realize these truths in their own hearts. The problem seems always to be "the other."

We can discourse all we want about racism, but until and unless we admit our own evil one to another, we can never solve this and all the other social problems that plague us.   Unfortunately for humans, I don't think we will ever find the courage to do so en masse. That is what it takes to be so vulnerable. We may do it, in the spirit of the following proverb, coined by whom I don't know: "After he has exhausted all other avenues, man acts wisely."

The last avenue that we may yet have to exhaust is the suffering of all humans on a scale never before seen by the world. This may be very close at hand. The type of suffering I am talking about here would level all remaining peoples to the only race there really is -- the human race.

January 29, 1995

Is Mental Illness A Myth?

ALTHOUGH MOST IN our world today largely treat mental illness as though it were an incontrovertible physical fact, like gravity, or, to use a better analogy, like cancer or diabetes, many believe it is a myth. Those who claim that mental illness is a myth do not claim that there are not "deviant, dangerous, and/or self-destructive behavior[s]" (Vatz, Weinberg, 1). They merely believe that the metaphors we use for behavior and thoughts should not be confused with physical illness processes (Vatz, Weinberg, 1).

As Theodore R. Sarbin states, "Any effort to criticize or clarify the concept of schizophrenia must begin from the position that 'schizophrenia' is a 'hypothetical construct' not a fact"(231). Again, as in Vatz and Weinberg, Sarbin, as a qualified psychiatrist in his day to day practice states that "[He] became aware of multifarious actions that were interpreted as 'presenting symptoms'--actions that family members or employers could not readily assimilate into their constructions of acceptable conduct" (232).

As far as research into the physical disorders (so-called brain diseases) that "cause" so-called mental illness, Szasz, in "Diagnoses are not diseases" sums up such research succinctly and wittily/satirically/sarcastically with this statement: "A screwdriver may be a drink or an implement. No amount of research on orange-juice-and-vodka can establish that it is a hitherto unrecognized form of a carpenter's tool" (1574). However, to slake the thirst of modern scholars (institutions of higher education) for formal scientific studies and statistics which they think "prove" things incontrovertibly, or at least dependably, following are some:

Professor James Manucuso along with Theodore Sarbin did exhaustive studies to review all research articles on Schizophrenia found in the Journal of Abnormal Psychology for 20 years starting in 1959 (Sarbin, 233). Part of their findings led them to "an unmistakable conclusion: that most schizophrenics cannot be differentiated from most normals on a wide variety of experimental tasks." Further, Sarbin states that, "At least since 1855, it has been noted that the diagnosis of insanity (later dementia praecox and schizophrenia) has been employed primarily as a diagnosis for poor people" (Sarbin, 234). (Sarbin is driving me batty with that passive language, e.g. "cannot be differentiated" rather than "the doctors could not differentiate most schizophrenics from most normals," and "has been employed as a" rather than "doctors have employed as a!") Finally, Sarbin states, "Despite its failure when examined by empirical methods, the social construction of schizophrenia has persisted. Its persistence is a function of the support it has received." In other words, the diagnosis of schizophrenia serves some powerful groups' interests, in spite of the fact that "[C]ountless [scientific] studies have not identified the disease entity" (Sarbin, 236).

Yet further, Sarbin states that most journal pieces use "statistically significant associations between. . .variables and diagnoses, not between. . .variables and conduct"

(237). It seems that Sarbin is saying that the arguments of many of these articles are circular in that they diagnose "disease" and then say that because of the diagnoses, the disease exists. He further states that "The conventional publication style facilitates the illusory conclusion that a cause or partial cause, of schizophrenia has been discovered" (237). (He did it again: "has been discovered" rather than "these scientists feel they have discovered!")

Sarbin and Manucuso's revelations about the sheer deception (mainly self-deception) that those who conducted these studies have perpetrated are myriad even throughout this short article. I have read a book by Sarbin on this same subject which goes into even greater detail. The other famous champion of the mental illness as myth sensibility that I have mentioned in this essay, Thomas Szasz, also compares and analyzes, not so much so-called objective clinical studies, but common sense thoughts on the matter. These often make sense to those given to thinking about the matter at all rather than seeing it as a forgone conclusion as our current Zeitgeist demands.

To give an idea of the penalty for committing heresy in the present era, I would like to quote a statement from Carol Iannone, "the embattled nominee to the Advisory Council of the National Endowment for the Humanities," from Vatz & Weinberg's article. I can clearly see why she is "the embattled nominee" and wonder how she ever got nominated in the first place while making such statements:

"[She] reviewed William Styron's book, *Darkness Visible*, describing his suffering from the 'disease' of depression. The review was skeptical of the notion of 'depression-as-disease.' She wrote that Styron's description of his emergence from depression makes one doubt that it is a disease without choice or a moral dimension. Styron, Iannone notes, states that, while in the throes of being enraptured by Brahms' 'Alto Rhapsody,' he steeled himself against an act (suicide) which would devastate his loved ones and constitute a 'desecration on myself.' 'What,' Iannone asked, 'were all his neurotransmitters and chemicals and hormones up to?' How she implied, could a disease be so amenable to the power of thought" (3)

Granted, many people today believe that the power of thought can overcome all kinds of physical diseases, which would not in this case support Ms. Iannone's conjecture. However, why did just her asking this question or contemplating this view bring what Vatz & Weinberg characterized as a "swift and vehement [reaction to Iannone's heresy]," from a Columbia University psychiatrist in an angry letter to the Washington Post's Commentary. This psychiatrist said, "How is it possible that, in the year 1990, one can still come across a person of considerable education (and literary erudition) who somehow has not learned that depression (and, most especially, suicidal depression) is a psychiatric illness, not primarily a moral dilemma or a mortal sin." I would not expect any psychiatrist to say any differently. One author, Robert Pirsig, who has written only two books on the subject, and, therefore, does not offer "sound" scientific research (except from the inside out!), so I am not really supposed to use him here, but I will, stated in his book, *Lila: An Inquiry Into Morals*, that if psychiatrists were to admit that people were not in need of psychiatrists' debatably "benevolent" care, what would be left for psychiatrists to do except find another profession (329)!

I, too, know this question from the inside out, as one of the so-called mentally ill. As Szasz states, most people who are branded as mentally ill, don't think they are; their families, the State, and other societal institutions which don't agree with them (in my case the church -- I don't believe in Jesus either, nor that he will save my soul -- look at all the other wretches who claim to believe in him and are not any better persons morally for it; not the most devoutly religious of them; and I'm going to believe in a god who can't even make his worshipers better? I don't think so!) think they are and stigmatize them as such. I, like Szasz, believe there are outlandish behaviors and thoughts, some of the latter, I hold, and some of the former, even I don't condone nor want to be around, but I do not consider them to be mental illness. This is a deep philosophical question of great magnitude, if more people would just take it up. The so-called mentally ill are mainly not able to take it up as they are so oppressed by those around them, not to mention what Szasz calls "mental straight jackets:" drugs. And those who could take it up are unwilling to, as they are unwilling to take up any question that might reveal truths about themselves or their world that they are unwilling to face.

April 1999

Works Cited

Pirsig, Robert. *Lila: An Inquiry Into Morals.* New York: Bantam, 1992.

Sarbin, Theodore R., *"Toward the Obsolescence of the Schizophrenia Hypothesis."* Taking Sides Clashing Views On Controversial Psychological Issues, 5th ed. Ed. Brent Slife. Guilford: Dushkin Publishing Group, 1996, pp. 222-230.

Szasz, Thomas S. *"Diagnoses are not diseases."* The Lancet, vol. 338: 12/21/28/91, pp. 1574-6.

---. *"What counts as disease?"* CMAJ (The Canadian Medical Association Journal), vol. 135, Oct. 15, 1986, pp. 859-860.

Vatz, Richard E., and Lee S. Weinberg. *"Is mental illness a myth?"* Expanded Academic ASAP. USA Today (Magazine). July 1993 v122 n578 p62(2). 19 Apr. 1999 <http://web4 searchbank.com/itw/session/597/105/11786413w5/10!bmk_1_0_ A13196291>.

Is There Such A Thing
As Mental Illness?

CONTRARY TO POPULAR belief, there are those who think that the question of the reality of mental illness is still debatable. The history of this debate seems, much to my surprise, to have started around the time of "The Enlightenment" or "The Age of Reason" beginning in approximately 1600 and spanning to approximately the end of the 1700's. I had always thought that madness (insanity) was an issue as far back as the time of Jesus or before. A quote from Askenasy's, *Are We All Nazis*, clears this up somewhat: "Had there been a lunatic asylum in the suburbs of Jerusalem, Jesus Christ would infallibly have been shut up in it at the outset of his public career. The interview with Satan on a pinnacle of the temple would alone have damned him, and everything that happened after could but have confirmed the diagnosis. The whole religious complexion of the modern world is due to the absence from Jerusalem of a lunatic asylum" (57, 58). In other words, the Zeitgeist of the world was quite different than it is today and than it became around 1600 as concerns so-called mental illness.

Klaus Doerner states in his book, *Madmen and the Bourgeoisie A Social History of Insanity and Psychiatry,* that the middle of the 17th Century saw the beginning in the West (Britain) of what he calls "the administrative sequestration of unreason (work houses, correctional institutions, etc.)" (15, 16). Before that and before the "Age of Reason" it seems there were no such things as "mental institutions" or "asylums" as we know them today. According to Thomas Szasz in the book he edited, *The Age of Madness the History of Involuntary Medical Hospitalization*, the furor has raged ever since, mainly between the so-called mad and their jailors as well as the rest of the institutions of society, e.g. their families, churches, police, etc.

Closer to our own time, there are the three main influences I have chosen to write mainly about here: Freud, Jung, and Szasz, respectively. Freud and his school of psychoanalysis, hailed in mainstream mental health circles as the founding father of modern psychology and the bedrock of most mainstream psychological practices, were the first to tackle the problem (issue, question, idea) of the unconscious, under that label: the unconscious. This idea developed from his practicing "free association" or "talking-out" which "provided him with a great deal of knowledge about the underlying causes of abnormal behavior" (Hall 15). I believe this so-called abnormal behavior is that which a client claims he or she cannot control and finds troubling in some way. I also believe that uncontrollable so-called abnormal thoughts which don't manifest in behavior but merely in states of mind which the client merely reported to Freud are included in this.

The unconscious to Freud was a repository of all the things inimical to consciousness as well as the dwelling place of his construct, the "id." Freud believed much like Jung did   that the "id" (like Jung's concept of the "collective unconscious") is "like the sea [oceanic, almost of limitless and unknown and unknowable depths]" and "contains everything." Further, Freud characterized the id almost exactly as Jung did the "collective unconscious:" "experiences that are repeated with great frequency and intensity in many individuals of successive generations become permanent deposits in the id... Not only is the id archaic from the standpoint of racial history, but it is also archaic in the life of the individual. It is the foundation upon which the personality is built" (Hall 27).

Freud concocted (or developed, as you will) a complex psychology with many variants. Hall states that according to Freud, "In the mentally healthy person these three systems [id, ego, superego] form a unified and harmonious organization. By working together co-operatively they enable the individual to carry on efficient and satisfying transactions with his environment. The purpose of these transactions is the fulfillment of man's basic needs and desires. Conversely, when the three systems of personality are at odds with one another the person is said to be maladjusted. He is dissatisfied with himself and with the world, and his efficiency is reduced" (Hall 22).

Although my writing may not be any better or clearer, this sounds like a bunch of nonsense to me. Were the Jews who were   persecuted by the Nazis "maladjusted?" Were the Nazis any less efficient? What are man's basic needs and desires? Food? Shelter? Sex? Love? Life, period? Different people say, and have said, different things down through the ages.

Some of the most creative people in history have been "dissatisfied with [themselves] and with the world," e.g. Virginia Woolf, Sylvia Plath, Vincent van Gogh, etc. Many may say that all of them were mentally ill because they all killed themselves, thwarting one of "man's basic needs and desires." But to be great of spirit (and when I say "to be great of spirit" I mean to possess many of what I consider to be the higher characteristics of human nature like sensitivity, compassion, perceiving deeper levels of reality; fuzzy concepts all, and hard to pin down, but most know them when they see them) from which spirit all great art, love, etc. comes while one is alive, is a much more basic need and even desire than longevity or waiting for one's life to end as some unseen hand dictates. Taking my own life is one thing I am too cowardly to do or I would have done so long ago, such is my grief about what I experience every day; I'm also very curious to see what happens next! I therefore think that to deem people who suffer deeply (often so those around them won't have to) and even die "from" their suffering (by their own hand) mentally ill, as Freud has done, is much more a moral/religious construct and verdict than a scientific premise congruant with any natural laws.

Now, on to Jung. I don't quite know how to characterize Jung. He too is considered one of the founding fathers of psychology with Freud (though not mainstream psychology as it is practiced today). Freud and Jung knew each other and were close associates for approximately six years. Jung departed from Freud over the question of libido or psychic energy only referring to sexual energy or dynamics as opposed to all psychic energy (Jung, *Memories, Dreams, Reflections* 208). He also felt that dreams were not mere facades that the unconscious had put up to obscure the meaning of the dream as did Freud, but that dreams as direct expressions of the unconscious, compensated the conscious attitude and merely "spoke" a different language than that of consciousness (Jung, *Modern Man In Search of a Soul* 20). Jung's school of psychoanalysis (which he called analytical psychology) is also very complex and has many components. Jung's psychology, however, both his personal psychology and his school of thought, allow a much greater breadth and scope to what is "normal" in the make-up of the human psyche.

In spite of this, Jung uses a lot of physical metaphors in describing his patients, including the words "sickness" and "ill" (Jung, *Modern Man In Search of a Soul* 39, 52). For instance, in giving an analogy for why he feels that dreams do not present facades behind which the real meaning of them lies, he states: "If sugar appears in the urine, then the urine contains sugar, and not albumen or urobilin or something else that I may have been led to expect" (Jung, *Modern Man in Search of a Soul* 6). Elsewhere he states that: "Just as the human body is a museum, so to speak, of its phylogenetic history, so too is the psyche" (*Archetypes of the Collective Unconscious* 287). These statements as well as others similar to it, may have started mainstream psychological institutions onto the path which led to the reification of what Jung always meant to be metaphor for states of mind and behavior and not exactly the same as physical diseases. Witness: "Despite the materialistic tendency to understand the psyche as a mere reflection or imprint of physical and chemical processes, there is not a single proof of this hypothesis" (*Archetypes of the Collective Unconscious* 57).

Although I believe that many of the mechanisms that Freud, and, especially, Jung postulate are true, e.g., in the case of Freud, repression, projection, identification, etc., and in the case of Jung, the collective unconscious and its archetypes, and myths as the collective "dreams" of nations and societies, etc., and can be signposts for counselors to help people with problems in living who want such help, I cannot agree that so-called neuroses or psychoses are on a par with physical illness. They simply are not treated the same in a social, moral, political or legal context. When I say treated, I am basically talking of the treatment accorded the carriers of, or people who are purported to have, these diseases. When one is physically ill there is rarely a stigma attached to one's disease and one is rarely blamed or ill-treated by one's relatives and associates and the other institutions of society because one is physically ill. Finally, and here is the rub, people who are physically ill are usually not forced to get treatment they don't want and must consent to their treatment unless they are unconscious.

This leads me to Thomas Szasz, another psychiatrist (1920-), who states emphatically in his article "Diagnoses are not diseases," published in the journal, *The Lancet*, that he became a psychiatrist specifically to debunk thinking that reifies metaphorical constructs about states of mind by taking them literally. Szasz does not deny that there are behaviors and states of mind that are "outrageous to common sense," and other conventions that society has established for getting meaning out of life, or contrary to what is socially acceptable. He however does not agree with the modern (over the past 40 years or so) "idea that every 'mental illness' will prove to be a brain disease" which "became increasingly accepted as a scientific fact" (1574).

I will summarize all these propositions with a quote from Szasz book, *The Manufacture of Madness A Comparative Study of the Inquisition and the Mental Health Movement*:

"In 'primitive' societies, men not only eat human flesh for its magical-symbolic characteristics, but also endow animals with human and superhuman qualities. In 'modern' societies, men do the reverse: they eschew eating human flesh, but endow persons with subhuman and animalistic qualities (for example, witches, Jews, madmen, et cetera.)

"The cannibal incorporates his victim to give himself virtue; we expel ours to give ourselves innocence. Ours is not only the more sophisticated, but perhaps also the graver, crime. And it is the crime that all of us, as a society, often require each other to commit. To refuse to persecute the socially accredited scapegoat is interpreted as an attack on society itself. This was clear during the Inquisition, in Nazi Germany, and on the West Coast of the United States between Pearl Harbor and the defeat of Japan. It is equally true today for the madman. To defend the rights of alleged mental patients is experienced as an attack on society...The fact that far more violence is committed against mental patients than by them does not matter. The action of the tribe, of the collective, of the State, is experienced as right; that of the independent individual wrong" (288).

April 1999

Bibliography

Askenasy, Hans. *Are We All Nazis?* Secaucus: L. Stuart, 1978.

Bandler, Richard. *Using Your Brain For A Change.* Moab: Real People Press, 1985.

Bradbury, Ray. *Farenheit 451.* New York: Ballantine Books, 1953.

Buckley, William F. Jr. *"Radical Insights on drug-taking."* Expanded Academic ASAP. National Review. Aug. 5, 1988 v40 n 15 p60(2). 19 Apr. 1999 <http//web4. searchbank.com /itw/session/597/105/11786413w5/ 24!bmk_3_0_A6542256>.

Doerner, Klaus. *Madmen and the Bourgeoisie A Social History of Insanity and Psychiatry.* New York: Basil Blackwell, 1981.

Freud, Sigmund. *The Psychopathology of Everyday Life.* Ed. James Strachey. New York: W. W. Norton & Co., 1965.

Goldman, M. J. *"Kleptomania: making sense out of nonsense."* American Journal of Psychiatry 1991; 148: 986-96.

Hall, Calvin S. *A Primer of Freudian Psychology.* New York: Mentor, 1982.

Holmes, Steven A. *"House Approves Bill Establishing Broad Rights For Disabled People."* New York Times 23 May 1990. late ed., sec. 1:1+.

Jung, Carl Gustav. *Collected Works.* Princeton: Princeton University Press, 1979.

Mancuso, James C. and Sarbin, Theodore R. Schizophrenia *Medical Diagnosis or Moral Verdict.* Elmsford: Pergamon Press, 1980.

Pirsig, Robert. *Lila: An Inquiry Into Morals.* New York: Bantam, 1992.

Postman, Neil. *Teaching As A Subversive Activity*. New York: Delacorte Press, 1969.

Ruggiero, Vincent Ryan. *The Art of Thinking*. New York: Longman, 1998.

St. Aubyn, Giles. *The Art of Argument*. New York: Taplinger Publishing Co.,   1985.

Schrag, Peter. *Mind Control*. New York: Delta, 1979.

Szasz, Thomas, ed. *The Age of Madness The Histroy of Involuntary Mental Hospitalization*. New York: Jason Aronson, 1974.

---. "*Diagnoses are not diseases*." The Lancet, vol. 338: 12/21/28/91, pp. 1574-6.

---. *The Manufacture of Madness A Comparative Study of the Inquisition and the Mental Health Movement*. New York: Harper Colophon Books, 1970.

---. *The Myth of Mental Illness*. New York: Hoeber-Harper, 1961.

---. *The Second Sin*. Garden City: Anchor Press, 1973.

---. *The Therapeutic State*. Buffalo: Prometheus Books, 1984.

---. *The Untamed Tongue A Dissenting Dictionary*. LaSalle: Open Court, 1990.

United States Code Annotated. *Americans With Disabilities Act*, Title 42, Secton 12211. Minneapolis: West Publications, 1995 updated 1998.

Vatz, Richard E., and Lee S. Weinberg. "*Is mental illness a myth?*" Expanded Academic ASAP. USA Today (Magazine). July 1993 v122 n578 p62(2). 19 Apr. 1999 <http://web4   searchbank.com/itw/session/597/105/11786413w5/10!bmk_1_0_ A13196291>.

Vonnegut Kurt. *God Bless You Mr. Rosewater*. New York: Henry Holt & Co., 1991.

Wells, H. G. *Fate of Man*. Alliance: Longman's, 1939.

African Religions

As MBITI STATES in his *African Religions and Philosophy*, "Over the whole of Africa, creation is the most widely acknowledged work of God" (39). Although the concept of an omnipotent, omniscient, omnipresent creator God is central to African Religions (with countless minor deities in tow, including the souls of the deceased, or "living-dead," as they are known) the religious life and observances of African Religions is "humanistic" or human centered (Mbiti 4, 5). As far as the duality between good and evil is concerned, especially its creation, Africans believe that God is wholly good and that all evil emanates from something other than God such as some part of his creation, e.g., some "living dead," spirits, and a principle of the personification of evil (much like monotheistic religions), that was once good, (as created by God), but took it upon itself to become evil (Mbiti 199).

I find this latter belief totally illogical in any believer, for if the former is true, that god is omnipotent and (especially) omniscient, if God didn't actually will (or create) the evil, It at least knew (omniscience) that the force that turned evil would do so. What kind of free will is that? This, though, seems typical to me of the almost total irrationality of most religious thought; how people come to these conclusions is beyond me. C. G. Jung's

Answer to Job, although also fanciful to some extent, at least looks squarely at what may be called "the dark side" of the deity as plainly   displayed in the "personality" of God as it is portrayed in many Biblical passages, especially those of Job, which are what Jung focusses on in his above-mentioned tome.

Some other instances of this line of reasoning about this in African religions are as follows: "According to some societies, individuals or the people as a body or through its chief or king, may offend against God. For example, the Barundi believe that God gets angry with a person who commits adultery. The Achwa believe that God punishes people who steal, neglect aging parents, murder or commit adultery. [Sounds like the Biblical Ten Commandments revisited!] The Bavenda say that if their chief offends against God, He punishes the whole people with locusts, floods or other calamities" (Mbiti 201).

This does not sound like a wholly good God to me; this God sounds demanding, and vindictive, attributes we would generally subsume under "the dark side" or "evil" were we considering any other (human) personality. In the above reference, I didn't see any evil deities or spirits at work in punishing and bringing about poetic justice to the offenders; the reference spoke only of the acts (punishment) of God. It seems, therefore, perhaps paradoxically, according to what people "supposedly" believe about God, that God does indeed visit evil upon those who do evil; "an eye for an eye, a tooth for a tooth, etc."

The impact of this dualistic principle, split off to be an "all good God" and an "all evil principle," so far as I can see, is to split the psyche of those who believe what

I consider to be this nonsense (in the literal meaning of that word "non-sense" or illogic as in getting lost somehow between the logical connections of one's premises by assuming certain things to be true when what precedes them is not, or at the very least doesn't make sense). If we see God in Its creation and we look at the creation squarely and brutally honestly, we see, especially in Africa, with the immense beauty of the creation (in the daytime anyway!) and its immensely horrifying aspects, like the sheer terror experienced at night in a jungle, death, the necessity that some must die in order that others may live (eating), disease, accidents, etc., all that we seemingly cannot control in nature, that God's creation reflects the maximum of beauty, as well as the maximum of horror. The one nowhere exists without the other. That should teach us about the nature of God/dess.

As Ernest Becker states in his *The Denial of Death*:

"What are we to make of a creation in which the routine activity is for organisms to be tearing others apart with teeth of all types--biting, grinding flesh, plant stalks, bones between molars, pushing the pulp greedily down the gullet with delight, incorporating its essence into one's own organization and then excreting with foul stench and gases the residue[?] Everyone reaching out to incorporate others who are edible to him. The mosquitos bloating themselves on blood, the maggots, the killer bees attacking with a fury and a demonism, sharks continuing to tear and swallow while their own innards are being torn out. . .Creation is a nightmare spectacular taking place on a planet that has been soaked for hundreds of millions of years in the blood of all its creatures. The soberest conclusion that we could make about what has actually been taking place on the planet for about three billion years is that it is being turned into a vast pit of fertilizer. But the sun distracts our attention, always baking the blood dry, making things grow over it, and with its warmth giving the hope that comes with the organism's comfort and expansiveness" (282, 283).

One last impact of the principle of dualism between good and evil, which I'm not sure if African religions has felt or not, we can derive from words the novelist W. Somerset Maugham placed into the mouth of a character who was a mystic in his *The Razor's Edge*: "[T]he world is not a creation, for out of nothing, nothing comes; but a manifestation of the eternal nature. . .evil is as direct a manifestation of the divine as good" (108), which dovetails nicely with all I have said above.

What the Africans have in common about the sacred is that they all believe in life after death, although "this does not constitute a hope for a future and better life," as Africans don't really have a concept for, and hence, have no belief in, the future, per se, at all. Africans also (sensibly I think) are what I have heard one writer call "Methodists," (though he wasn't speaking about Africans, but people who are born with the influence of the planet Mercury strong in their horoscopes) meaning that they believe that their good is here on Earth, right now, not in some distant place (heaven) and time (the future) (Mbiti 4). As Mbiti states (badly using the passive verb tense, as he does throughout the book, I might add): "There is neither paradise to be hoped for nor hell to be feared in the hereafter" (4). Further,

"[t]he soul of man does not long for spiritual redemption [in African religions], or for closer contact with God in the next world. . .There is no messianic hope or apocalyptic vision with God stepping in at some future moment to bring about a radical reversal of man's normal life. God is not pictured in an ethical-spiritual relationship with man. Man's acts of worship and turning to God are pragmatic and utilitarian rather than spiritual or mystical" (Mbiti 4, 5).

Life on Earth and after death depend on humans through live humans committing acts of propitiation, such as prayers, libations, offerings of food, and animal sacrifice to the "living-dead," or ancestors, which living-dead I have otherwise briefly noted previously (Mbiti 81). These are done unto five generations of ancestors because the Africans believe that their ancestors to five generations are not fully dead yet and need these services to be remembered and to intercede for the living with God and other spirits (Mbiti 82). The living-dead may protect or warn living people of calamities that can help keep the living safe. The way the living-dead accomplish these warnings is through appearing to the living in visions or dreams; the living dead usually approach the elders of their family in this way. Africans believe that their living-dead speak both human language and the language of God. This because they have recently departed human life and are approaching closer to the spiritual realm of God. If the living neglect the living-dead, the Africans believe that the latter may become angry and visit them with "misfortunes and sufferings" (Mbiti 82).

According to Mbiti, Africans do not consider the above "ancestor worship," but just a sort of respect and honor as in keeping the memory of the living-dead alive, as Americans or Europeans might do by placing pictures, flowers, or other memorials (even tombstones) on the graves of their loved ones. Africans do not consider their activities in relation to their deceased loved ones ancestor worship, anymore than we consider ours to be so (Mbiti 8, 9). As we can see, for Africans, the relatively smooth running of their world depends on relationships between humans and "the spirit world" in all the latter's forms, from the "living-dead," to the other spirits, to the highest of the high, God.

The economy of Africa had traditionally been mainly barter and not a monetary economy. With the "detribalization" of Africa, to use Mbiti's term, one basis of African traditional religions, their attachment to the land, to which Mbiti states that the Africans were "mystically bound," and through the break-up of the family due to revolutionary industrialization, e.g. colonization, Christianity, diamond digging, etc., the religious traditions of Africa have, in many ways, been turned upside down. This leaves many Africans rootless and dehumanized (214).

As we know, these last are not new phenomena, but are a continuation of history through the ages. Ernest Becker quoted Freud in his The Denial of Death thus: ". . .I have found little that is 'good' about human beings on the whole. In my experience most of them are trash, no matter whether they publicly subscribe to this or that ethical doctrine or none at all. . .If we are to talk of ethics, I subscribe to a high ideal from which most of the humans beings I have come across depart most lamentably" (qtd. in Becker 256). I don't know if Freud included himself among those who, even though they may be the best of the best of people, are still lamentably off the mark; I consider myself to be so. All we can strive for is excellence (although unfortunately, most do not even strive for that); the rest, the overwhelming abundance of evil that befalls both man and beast from both man and nature, is a mystery that we all participate in, but that none can gainsay.

August, 2000

Works Cited

Becker, Ernest. *The Denial of Death*. New York: The Free Press, 1973.

Maughm, W. Somerset. *The Razor's Edge*. New York: Penguin Books, 1963.

Mbiti, John S. *African Religions and Philosophy*. New Hampshire: Heinemann, 1999

Eternal versus Ephemeral
Elements in Religious Thought

IT SEEMS THAT, as ever (eternal), where the majority is, that is where the dominant religious ideas are and minority religious concepts are usually routed out, or, at the very least, suppressed. Majority cultures have done this either through superior brute force of arms and wholesale destruction of the minority and, as in more modern times, in combination with subtler forms of persecution. Either way, the result is the same: suppression of minority religious forms, as well as assimilation of those very forms into the majority religion.

For example, when Christianity was a minority religious concept in ancient Rome, its adherents were physically tortured and put to death. Even its founder, Jesus, was put to death for espousing the heresy that he was a god. And right from the start, Christianity based its philosophy on older pagan (then majority) forms. Witness from Joseph Campbell's and Bill Moyers' *The Power of Myth*:

> Moyers: So when the Council of Ephesus met in the year 431 after the death of Christ, and proclaimed Mary to be the Mother of God, it wasn't the first time.

> Campbell: No, in fact that argument had been going on in the Church for some time. But the place where this

decision was made, at Ephesus, happened at that time to be the greatest temple city in the Roman empire of the Goddess Artemis, or Diana. And there is a story that when the council was in session, arguing this point, the people of Ephesus formed picket lines and shouted in praise of Mary, "The Goddess, the Goddess, of course she's the Goddess."

Well, what you have then in the Catholic tradition is a coming together of the patriarchal, monotheistic Hebrew idea of the Messiah as one who is to unite the spiritual and temporal powers, and the Hellenistic, classical idea of the Savior as the dead and resurrected son of the Great Goddess by a virgin birth. *There were plenty of such saviors reborn* (emphasis mine) (180).

In more modern times, Christianity having become the majority religion, it's adherents much more subtly, though no less effectively, suppress or invalidate, more mystical nature based religious ideas, a special case in point being Native American Religions. The adherents of Christianity do this by deeming all religious ideas outside of their own as not true, or more specifically, the work of *their* devil.

One eternal element about religion, then, seems to be persecution of minority religious ideas, while one ephemeral element is how religions incorporate other religious ideas into their own. Sam Gill gives an example of the latter in *Native American Religions* in the case of how the Yaqui Indians assimilated many Christian religious forms such as dramatic pageantry in their Easter celebrations (150-155).

Another eternal element of religions is the similarity of their ideas (mythologies and stories, even cosmologies) in spite of their many differences. Gill demonstrates these similarities over various Native American religions when he discusses the story of the Seneca Tribe's Creator Twins, and notes that, "This type of story is known among [Native American] tribes all over North America" (20). What's more, not only is that type of story (myth) familiar in Native American religions, but in all cultures; and if not that type of story, then others.

Another type of story that is similar down through the ages in all religions is that of the hero. Gill explains one hero story among Native American tribes as encompassing, "the adventures of the heroes, the consequences of their failures, and their resulting travail and misfortunes," and I would add, their final triumph over adversity (22). The story of the hero is the central theme also of Christianity, in the suffering and eventual triumph over death of Jesus. As Joseph Campbell so eloquently puts it, "When Jesus says, 'He who drinks from my mouth will become as I am and I shall be he,' he's talking from the point of view of that being of beings, which we call the Christ, who is the being of all of us. Anyone who lives in relation to that is as Christ. Anyone who brings into his life the message of the Word is equivalent to Jesus. . ." (213). The hero quest is ever glorious and it is ever perilous, as well as the same in its essentials.

This is so because as Joseph Campbell again puts it more eloquently than I ever could, "The psyche is the inward experience of the human body, which is essentially the same in all human beings, with the same organs, the same instincts, the same impulses, the same conflicts, the same fears. Out of this common ground have come what Jung has called the archetypes, which are the common ideas of myths. . ." (51). These are the similar stories and ideas that humans tell and have regardless of what different cultures or religious spheres they come from in all epochs of time.

As you can tell from my survey above of the eternal vs. the ephemeral in religion, I don't see nearly as much that is ephemeral as I do that is eternal in religious expression. Although we have now moved into a new century and are flush with wondrous technology of all descriptions, nature (which includes humanity) is ever the same, especially interior nature. Whether it will change much (or whether we will or can change it much) only time will tell.

October, 2000

Works Cited

Campbell, Joseph, with Moyers, Bill. *The Power of Myth*.
  New York: Doubleday, 1988.
Gill, Sam D. *Native American Religions An Introduction*.
  Belmont: Wadsworth, 1982.

Astro/Psycho/Religio Theories of Human Nature/Behavior

THERE ARE MANY theories about the ways people relate to others, such as one-to-one, in groups, emotionally, as leaders, etc., including, astrological, psychological, and philosophical theories. Some believe that the ways people relate to others are direct expressions of innate character such as industriousness and/or guilt as opposed to laziness and/or sensuality, honesty as opposed to deception, compassion as opposed to selfishness. Others feel that these ways of relating are more shaped by the environment. Yet others feel the ways we relate are shaped by both our innate characters and our environments. The following thoughts about some of these theories did not come to me just from reading "Critical Period Hypothesis" in Smith's *Bridging The Gap* (20-23). I have been pondering about and wondering at these possibilities for the past twenty years and must admit that I wrote the draft for this paper for the first time five and a half years ago as a means of expressing my thoughts on these factors of influence of which I was (and am still) so in awe.

It seems that nature (or inner factors) have to do with nurture (or environment) in the above- mentioned pairs of opposites of character traits, for, as in all pairs of opposites, each pole (or opposite tendency) shares some similarity with its partner. To illustrate the above, I will tell of a baby I once observed whose astrological sign is Libra who seemed to always be "relating" to one person at a time in her daily environment. One of the sign Libra's strongest traits is that people born under that sign are good at relating to people one-to-one. This one-to-one relating, however, would not seem to necessarily have any bearing on the content or tenor of those relationships, although perhaps her innate character would.

Being surrounded by groups of people might not necessarily have an affect on the tenor of her relationships either, nor whether or not these relationships would dispose her toward expressing the positive aspects or the negative aspects of Venus and the sign Libra. (Venus is the planet that astrologers believe influences the sign Libra.) The baby's orientation of relating to people one-to-one, whether in a lazy, sluttish way, or in graceful and refined ways seems as though it will be influenced by the environment.

As I stated above in my understanding that all pairs of opposites participate in each other to some degree (and as astrological lore tells us), this environment will probably influence our youngster toward some of the positive aspects of her astrological sign and planet at some times and toward some of the negative aspects at others. We, of course, cannot know whether or not her innate character (if there is such a thing; I believe there is) will influence her more or less than her environment in the expression of the above-mentioned traits, but it is something to ponder. Finally, in this vein, many believe that all this astrological talk is speculation, but in my defense, I will say that I am an astrologer of some thirty years study and practice. I therefore believe that astrology is a valid viewpoint for pondering and wondering about the tendencies that shape human nature and behavior both from without and within, as I hope I have shown above.

Some people have one kind of environment while others, even in the same family, have a different one. Examples of situations which would illustrate this are: children born many years apart to the same parents; families where the parents' economic situation changes for better or worse with different children which affect the parents' behavior and parenting styles from child to child; parents projecting different aspects of themselves onto their various offspring, thus affecting the parents' attitudes and behavior differently toward different children; ad infinitum.

I am not sure if we can prove the astrological, psychological, or philosophical points of view for all cases which fall into categories such as suicides or other human behavior, motivations, moods, and attitudes as with some other law of nature like gravity. One psychologist, B. F. Skinner, developed a theory that there is no such thing as consciousness or interiority, no matter how distasteful that is to our usual way of thinking and perceiving. What he might have said, is that the way we perceive certain realities, is a consequence of the names we have given them, and using those names rather than others.

For instance, when we use the word or name "schizophrenia" for the reality of the unconventional behavior that we as family members, policemen, psychiatrists, and other administrators of the institutions of society do not approve of in certain people, we do not necessarily know the true nature of the origins or motives of those people's behavior. However, once we name these people's behavior in this way, we can justify many cruel and heartless behaviors toward them, although based on the fact that it is we who are disgusted and distressed by their behavior most times, not they who are. The true nature of most of the realities we give names to, therefore, including giving the diagnosis of schizophrenia to unacceptable behavior as though it were something other than that, i.e., a physical disease, have not nearly as much as we may wish to do with what we name these realities at all.

I guess because of the enormity of the whole question, both in largeness and grotesquery, of whether we are most affected by nature or nurture, the vast majority of people take the philosopher, Hume's position. Hume believed that since we can't understand the "whys" and "wherefores" of the larger more perplexing questions about human nature, like, "Why are we here?" "Does each person have an individual purpose?" we might as well unquestioningly join the majority of people by uncritically following our emotions in lives dedicated to action with little forethought or reflection (236). So many people do this, even those with the highest credentials and education, that there is no one who can doubt that this is the only thing to do without risking ostracism and persecution.

The final thought I have on the subject of what shapes human nature for different humans is that in the end this whole subject is an ineffable mystery, the answer to which is to be found in some distant future or never at all; we can only speculate and stand in awe of the unknown (unknowable?) about our own beings.

1999

Works Cited

Reese, W.L., *Dictionary of Philosophy and Religion*, Atlantic HIghlands: Humanities Press Inc., 1980.

Smith, Brenda D., *Bridging the Gap*, New York: Longman, 1997.

Mysticism Through the
Interpretive Lens of an Insider

A PARTIAL DEFINITION of mysticism is: "a spiritual and non-discursive (unchanging) approach to the union of soul with God, or whatever is taken to be the central reality of the universe." This is from W. L. Reese's reference work, *Dictionary of Philosophy and Religion Eastern and Western Thought*. This is a partial definition from this source. However, it brings the meaning of mysticism to its essential core in all its different traditions. These traditions include Hinduism, the religious traditions of ancient Greece, Gnosticism (Christian), Sufism (Islamic), Cabala [Kabbalah] (Jewish), and Roman Catholic Mysticism. I am relatively familiar with all of the above-named mystical traditions. I consider myself to be a mystic of the most universalistic stripe. I feel that I have had compelling mystical experiences of my connection with the godhead. This, mainly in an immanent or inward sense.

"The shaman [which could also be considered a type of mystic, or at least which I consider to be so] is the person, male or female, who in his[/her] late childhood or early youth has an overwhelming psychological experience that turns him[/her] totally inward. It's a kind of schizophrenic crack-up. The whole unconscious opens up, and the shaman falls into it." Joseph Campbell stated this in his book, *The Power of Myth*. This book came from transcripts of a PBS program with Bill Moyers. That is what happened to me at age 20. It began with less intensity at approximately age 18.

At that time, I started having dreams that were more like visions. My consciousness turned from almost total concern with what was outside of me, e.g., friends, family, social life, etc., to being almost totally concerned with what went on inside of me, e.g., dreams, intense studies of metaphysics, etc., to the point where I felt totally different than how I used to be. This felt strange to me, and I tried to shake it off. I have not been able to do so to this day!

Had I been living in an aboriginal tribe, upon exhibiting such behavior, I would most likely have been taken to the nearest shaman/ess and apprenticed to him/her. However, this is modern-day America. I was carted off to the nearest mental clinic.

I find myself to be, and notice that other people find me to be so numinous or charismatic (meaning "magnetic" as in being extremely "attractive" to people's positive or negative feelings, thoughts, aspirations, detractions, etc.), that the following saying applied to the personage known to most as Jesus Christ applies to me, as well: "Had there been a lunatic asylum in the suburbs of Jerusalem, Jesus Christ would infallibly have been shut up in it at the outset of his public career. The interview with Satan on a pinnacle of the temple would alone have damned him, and everything that happened after could but have confirmed the diagosis. The whole religious complexion of the modern world is due to the absence from Jerusalem of a lunatic asylum." This is quoted in Hans Askenasy's book, *Are We All Nazis*, on page 58.

In any event, I have many experiences which are horrifying. These consist of both the ways people treat (persecute) me because of my difference, and because of my own thoughts and feelings in connection with same. I continue to study in the midst of this. I continue to ponder.

When I was 26, approximately 6 to 8 years after this initial upheaval, I was at a Christmas party with my family. We had partitioned ourselves off into small groups for private conversations. I was sitting with a favorite male cousin of mine. He is highly educated and intellectual. The two are not necessarily the same. He was at the time studying to become a medical doctor. He is an atheist. He stated to me at that time, that he did not believe that Jesus was (is) the son of God.

Well, I found that to be sheer blasphemy! I did not dare mention it to other family members. I did not mention it to anyone! I could not conceive that people could even think such things! However, as that anecdote's appearance in this essay attests, it stayed with me.

I came upon many books in my studies. To mention just two, Donovan Joyce's, *The Jesus Scroll*, and Elaine Pagels', *The Gnostic Gospels*. I came upon Pagels' book much later than Joyce's. The edition of Joyce's book that I own is now a very valuable rare book. These books, and many others, as well as my cousin's above-mentioned comment, and my horrific experiences at the hands of my compatriots, jarred me out of my complacently held exoteric Christian beliefs.

I went through a period of believing that Christ is a consciousness, not a historical personage. This is a mystical belief I still hold. I also became much surer of my own divinity, as well as everyone else's. This is in spite of the fact that the majority of everyone else does not realize their own divinity. I mean this in the direct sense of making the knowledge of this unassailably real (conscious) inside themselves. I am much surer of this than I am of the supposed historical existence of the personage most know as Jesus. I am therefore less sure of his divinity in any other way than of mine or anyone else's.

Next, through my exhaustive reading, I have come to believe that the quintessence of the godhead is pure being. This includes especially its feminine aspect. The godhead does nothing. In yet other words, it does not act at all. It does not love. It does not punish. It simply IS. It is in everything. It is the underlying condition for the existence of everything. It need be no more.

When I say these words, I feel as though I am saying nothing that would be intelligible to almost anyone I know. Most of those in my social circle are extremely uneducated. This leads to them being very concrete in their thinking, having very few general ideas. To put it kindly, they're very simple-minded to me. Orwell described his concept of "the proles" this way in his book, *1984*. He stated that they can be given freedom of thought because they don't think.

I rarely try anymore to describe what I understand a mystic to be. I also rarely try to explain what I understand about my godhead or the godhead of these people, to these people. I rarely try to do it even when they ask me to. Unfortunately, even with the best of understanding on both sides, it is hard to describe this reality because it is ineffable, indescribable.

I feel that I've had several mystical experiences. Not the least of which was a mystical, sexual union with a man I love. For, unlike the exoteric (outer forms of) tradition of the mainly monotheistic religions, I don't see nature as something that is beneath humans or inferior to spirit. It is all one to me. I, therefore, tend to see what is most natural to me, such as enjoying sexual pleasures with one I love, whether I may be married to him or not as long as we are both single, to be as spiritual a practice as praying or fasting or other nature denying religious practices might be to more traditional religious observers.

I do add the reservation that my natural behaviors must not interfere with those of others. I can also see where many people could feel that what I might consider not interfering with the rights of others would not be what they would consider so. However, that is not within the scope of this essay. I, therefore, won't go into a long digression about it. I will just let it stand as it is.

One of the most impressive mystical experiences I've ever had happened to me several years ago. I don't remember the exact date. It seemed to take place outside of time. I left my apartment on a beautiful June afternoon. The sun was shining gloriously. It was just the right temperature for me. The birds were singing. There was a soft breeze blowing.

I walked one block from the building where I live to a park. When I reached the entrance of the park, I looked down the path I was approaching. It has trees on either side. At that time of year, they were in full bloom. The foilage met in the middle forming a semi-canopy over the path. It was just a glorious day and scene!

Right before I entered onto the path, I seemed to go out of myself. I felt a connection with everyone and everything around me. It was a mute, absolutely wordless understanding. It was truly an ecstatic feeling, in the literal sense of the word. I was outside myself and outside of time. This feeling lasted only a few moments. Then I was back in the beautiful day. I still felt its beauty, but had lost the intensity of my inner connection with it. However, to this day, I remember the experience vividly emotionally. When I think about it, briefly I am there again in that state! James Redfield writes vividly about such a state in his book, *The Celestine Prophecy*.

One of the drawbacks of this type of revealed experience is, as I have stated above, it is largely ineffable. One cannot fully explain it in words. Although one is in an extreme state of realization of being at-one with everyone and everything, it can also be very separative because of its ineffable nature. The best way to understand it is to experience it oneself. However, one cannot always make it happen. I didn't.

Further, this separativeness has led in my life to my fellows generally ostracizing and persecuting me because I am different. This began for me at a very young age, even before these experiences. This has largely frustrated my need for social fulfillment. This is very hard at times. That because I am not in a constant state of ecstasy and have more mundane needs like anyone else.

In moments of serenity, I accept this as my destiny and wonder what it portends for the future. At times I am hopeful, at others despairing. I think I have developed inwardly to an astronomical degree. That is because of what I have suffered and what I have learned. Sometimes, I think that the latter has made it all worthwhile. Sometimes, I think that if I could live a so-called "normal" life, I would give up all that I know and have experienced of its (my) inner greatness. Right now the jury is out. To paraphrase Herodotus: "Call no man happy til you see his end."

May, 2000

Works Cited

Askenasy, Hans. *Are We All Nazis?* Secaucus: L. Stuart, 1978.

Bartlett, John. *Familiar Quotations*. Boston: LIttle Brown & Company, 1955.

Campbell, Joseph, w. Moyers, Bill. *The Power of Myth*. New York: Doubleday, 1988.

Joyce, Donovan. *The Jesus Scroll*. Melbourne: Ferret Books, 1972.

Orwell, George. *1984*. New York: Harcourt Brace Jovanovich, Inc., 1949.

Paden, William E. *Interpreting the Sacred*. Boston: Beacon Press, 1992.

Pagels, Elaine. *The Gnostic Gospels*. New York: Vintage Books, 1979.

Reese, W. L. *Dictionary of Philosophy and Religion Eastern and Western Thought*. Atlantic Highlands: Humanities Press, 1980.3

Reading "Why Handguns Must Be Outlawed"

Although the above-mentioned article has many fallacies in logic (almost anything we read does) it is no better or worse than much other writing I read that attempts to persuade, including my own. I often look for fallacies (or errors in logic and fact) in what I read, write, and in what other people say to me, and I often find them. However, I do not tend to think "critically" as *Bridging the Gap* describes critical thinking and as I have seen others describe it before. I do not always rely on facts and statistics and noted and well-documented and credentialled experts to come to my conclusions.

In defense of my way of thinking, which, in a word, I would term, creative, or even mystical, I believe that thinking without blending the best of feeling makes one into the kind of thinker who reveres science as one's secular religion as does the member of organized religion make the dogma/canon of his/her sacred beliefs. There are still many people who feel this way although most supposedly highly educated people believe that we as a civilization are beyond all that.

For instance, although statistics can tell us about some facets of reality, they can also be damned nonsensical!

There is a cartoon in a book called *The Far Side Gallery 3* by Gary Larson where a mother introduces her 1.5 children (someone's statistical average of how many children American nuclear families have) and there is a picture of a whole child and half a child looking at TV: absurd! Also, to paraphrase C. G. Jung, who said in his book, *The Undiscovered Self*, if you have a pebble bed consisting of 200 pebbles and you weigh them all and decide from your statistical calculations that the average pebble weighs 2 oz., there may still not be a single pebble in the bunch which weighs 2 oz.!

Jung further stated that a million zeros added together (as in mass man congregating together to make themselves feel that they are more than they are or could possibly be alone) still do not make one (or one individual or organism); in other words, people as a group have no reality, only the individuals in a group are carriers of reality. In spite of these facts, those who wield statistics become highly irritated and piqued (emotional!) if you dispute the above with them, which shows me that they are as much fanatics in the grip of their secular canon and are as true believers as any fanatic in the grip of his/her sacred religion.

Finally, I would like to quote Vincent Ruggiero, author of *The Art of Thinking*, who states that "[t]ruth is what is so about something, the reality of the matter, as distinguished from what people wish were so, believe to be so, or assert to be so." This being the case (and I have puzzled over this matter incessantly, as someone who has experienced many bizarre levels of reality as well as what people wish, and assert to be so about same, and have come to the conclusion that Ruggiero's statement about truth is the case), it is not the truth's problem to draw nearer to human beings, but humans' responsibility to draw nearer the truth.

To do that, one needs not only critical thinking (or cold, hard logic and facts), which the many writers of college text books, including Smith in her *Bridging the Gap*, believe to be paramount in this searching for, finding, and judging the value of truth, but the courage to go where the premises lead you regardless of the expedience (or advantage, or inexpediency or disadvantage) of going there, for one. Unfortunately, since most college textbooks give no basis for such courage (Ruggiero's being an exception) the problem of reaching truth and valuing it will remain a problem until more of them (as well as the teachers who rely upon them) do!

1999

Works Cited

Jung, Carl Gustav. *The Undiscovered Self.* Boston: Little Brown, 1958.

Larson, Gary. *The Far Side Gallery 3.* Kansas City: Universal Press Syndicate, 1988.

Lee, Donna. *Knowing.* Jamaica: MYSTICSOURCE, 1996.

Ruggiero, Vincent Ryan. *The Art of Thinking A Guide to Crical and Creative Thought.* 5th ed. New York: Longman, 1998.

Smith, Brenda. *Bridging the Gap.* 5th ed. New York: Longman, 1997.

Dear Professor Trela

THIS MAY BE unusual, but I wanted to write to you after dropping your class today to give you better reasons why I did so:

From the first time I spoke with you, I got the impression that you were not interested in what I had to say or thought nearly as much as you were interested in imparting to me what you think and what you think you know. I deplore this trait in anyone which is why my associates are a paltry few. When I mentioned my disappointment in you to my mentor, David Elliott, he told me that you were the most popular mentor (either in History or in the school). This really made me dead set against you! For, for one to be that popular, one must be either wholly operating under the Zeitgeist of this present time, which is one of utter decadence, or must be compromising himself something awful, which amounts to about the same thing.

Two statements you made in your "Welcome to World History One:" "You are about to embark on an exciting journey visiting the world's great civilizations in the pre-modern era;" and "While no one can ever predict the future, men and women can look to the past to gain important insights and develop perspective to help them understand what may lie ahead," were both made as foregone conclusions which many other students who are not as used to thinking for themselves and questioning authority will probably believe as forgone conclusions because they would like to pass your course. I would like to decide for myself what I find exciting, and I have been predicting the future (accurately) for quite a long time now, i.e., I predicted every president who entered office since 1980 (except for Bill Clinton; I thought that people would not go for his moral outrages, but they seem to be very popular and cause for celebration in our society these days from its lowest sinks to its highest echelons) and some Governors and Mayors too -- and not from any polls; just from using my intuition and from little remarks the candidates had made. If you choose to call this fortune telling (like your example of "someone telling you you're going to walk outside and discover a pot of gold and that's not going to happen;" it has happened, and does happen every day, it may never happen to you because you don't believe it can or have not earned it [karma] or otherwise don't deserve it!), that choice simply shows your lack of respect for (and even ignorance of) the beliefs of people other than yourself or other than our modern high-priesthood called science.

For, how many people have directly and personally experienced half the scientific truths or laws or discoveries that this very state religion tells us are so? Not many! Most of us take completely on faith what we are told about most diseases, and other scientific discoveries -- all of which simply are not true as doctors and scientists have vested interests to protect just like everybody else and are not paragons of virtue just because they entered into those fields; often the opposite is true.

Witness Robert Pirsig from his *Lila: An Inquiry Into Morals:* "Phaedrus had always believed science is a search for truth. A real scientist is not supposed to sell out that goal to corporations who are searching for mere profit. Or, if he had to sell out in order to live that was nothing to be happy about. These fraternity brothers of his acted like they never heard of science as truth." Finally, in that vein, I do not respect those who do not respect me, I don't care what their titles or positions.

Another position you took in regard to the Gilgamesh Epic with the same obstinate lack of looking at a broader point of view (at least you didn't mention it to me) was that the city triumphed over the country because they were "more organized." This seems a euphemistic way to say because they were more ruthless, wanton, and power hungry, just like city folk today.

I am no nature woman, although my hair and face go unadorned at almost all times and are in their natural state except for daily grooming, but I can at least appreciate that country dwellers, in a word, nature, is something that I should respect and be in awe of as though it is my mother, and nurturer, in spite of its awesome power to devastate my life in its capricious violence, and that I am in and of nature (especially as a woman) and not in a position to control or subdue it (I am definitely not an engineer, nor do I have that mindset). I think it is horrendous that a college professor of World History should be so steeped in his own time as you are as to be almost completely gobbled up in its Weltanschauung, and, again, Zeitgeist!

I recall having one teacher once who truly respected me, and my thoughts and feelings in spite of the fact that she disagreed strongly with me and my marks in her class reflected same. This I would not expect from you nor anyone who presents himself to me as you do. I also do not expect you to think any differently from reading this letter as that is a rarity I find among my correspondents akin to my ability to physically fly to the Moon!

Finally, I will give one more anecdote which point of view I have always subscribed to, that I found in one of my textbooks for another CDL course, then I will sum up for you what the topic, major details, and main idea of this letter are, since your school seems to find that such an important way to understand what one reads; I wouldn't want you to miss a thing!:

"Most of the Plains Indians believed that land could be utilized but never owned. The idea of owning land was as absurd as owning the air people breathed. To some, the sacredness of the land made farming against their religion. Chief Somohalla of the Wanapaun explained why his people refused to farm. "You ask me to plow the ground! Shall I take a knife and tear my mother's bosom?. . .You ask me to cut grass and make hay and sell it, and be rich like white men! But how dare I cut off my mother's hair?"

James Kirby Martin et al.,
America and Its People

Topic: Why I chose to drop World History I.
Major Details: I think you are a sell out and therefore are very popular and never even think about this; disrespectful as a forgone conclusion about beliefs other than your own or those of the present Zeitgeist; would not be a teacher who would meet my needs. Main Idea: Don't

be such a bone-head! Don't let your   thought patterns become like cement so that you can't change and grow as you are asking your students to do, and you might find your intuition awakening and you, yes, even you, might be able to predict the future!

Yours sincerely,

Donna Lee

January 27, 1999
I received absolutely no response.

My Most Important Learning Goals

I DO NOT always know when I'm learning! The process of learning can be unconscious for me in that I do not consciously consider that when I receive answers to certain questions I ask, for instance, that I am learning. Hence, my learning goals are relatively vague. In spite of that, I will try to describe some of my learning goals.

One of my most important learning goals is to learn how to stop "writing or English professionals," such as teachers (especially English teachers), professional editors, publishers, and the like from criticizing my writing abilities so harshly and so personally. I have received this extreme criticism ever since I started college in 1976 regardless of whether I worked hard and did my best on the papers so judged, or just threw them off with little thought. The latter was rare. I would like to do this because I find this criticism to be not only unfeeling, but unfair! It is really painful. I feel that I am an excellent writer, and when lay people read my work, some of them intelligent, avid readers, they all praise my work; usually more than it deserves, I think.

I feel that I am relatively objective about my writing ability. For, as science has proven (relatively), objectivity is, at best, relative. Sometimes we can have more, and sometimes less. I don't know if being more objective is a natural trait or if one can learn it. I have always been somewhat objective about myself. By saying this I mean that I can stand at least somewhat outside of myself and reflect on who and how I am and accurately judge same. To explain this trait further, I will give an example of objectivity or stepping outside one's natural (usually euphemistic) way of viewing oneself that I came across in an early college anthropology course:

There were once a people called the Nacirema. Our anthropologist who was totally foreign to (outside of and objective to) the Nacerima noticed that they had all kinds of odd (or what seemed so to her) religious rituals, especially ablutions. Every day, usually in the morning and the evening, the Nacirema would go into rooms they had set aside especially for these ablutions in their dwellings and close themselves completely off from their fellows for at least an hour to privately do these rituals. These rituals seemed to include washing the body thoroughly, including the teeth and gums and other ritual grooming. Our anthropologist, of course, couldn't be sure about all that the Naricema did in these religious rituals because each member usually did them alone and strictly in private, although some might go to the "ablution room" together.

There was more to the story that I don't remember. Have you guessed that Naricema is American spelled backward, and that that story is how American's might look to someone who stood totally outside of our way of life? If you find it hard to imagine who might view us like this, imagine someone from a third world country, or a different epoch in time. She might see what we do in the bathroom (called "ablution room" above) as mysterious religious rituals which we take totally for granted because we are so subjectively immersed in our way of life and rarely stand outside ourselves at all.

This is just one example. It is the clearest one I could find. Another, which may not be as clear, is what I understand to be the fact that I am hardly a writer up to the standards of those novelists, raconteurs, and storytellers I most admire like Mary Renault, Graham Greene, John Updike, and the list goes on and on, no matter what the lay people who admire my work say. At least not in the form of novels. However, I also do not need any college courses to tell me about grammar, syntax, etc.

When a "professional" writer (I guess this means he/she gets paid for his/her writing efforts) tells me that the holier-than-thou tone of a paper that only two people (him/her and my professor) are going to see will "turn people off," I find that almost totally biassed and unobjective and unprofessional on the level of criticism. Unfortunately for me, the vast majority of the people I come into contact with tend to judge me thus and to be unobjective in the same manner. This is the bane of my existence and is what caused me to cut off my college education in my earlier years which crippled me professionally. The same has been the case since I started back to school with Empire State College, and to tell the truth, I don't know how to stem this tide. It seems beyond me. The above-mentioned goal, to stop this criticism, does not seem to be within my means. I have been trying to stop it with every means at my disposal since it began. It has truly beaten me.

The other learning goal I have is to, at the very least, attain my associate degree from Empire State College. If I have to continue under the above regime, that goal will prove difficult, and may even prove impossible. I am not one to shrink from impossible seeming odds or I would have been a suicide a long time ago rather than sitting here (surviving) writing this paper. The fact, however, that I have come this far proves to me that in spite of the great odds I perceive are against me, I can possibly, with tenacity and every other resource I have at my command, succeed. I have the time management skills, and other skills necessary to do a laudatory job in completing my education. I will use them as long as I find the struggle worthwhile. With a little luck and all of the above-mentioned skills (resources), I hope to make it past the above-mentioned obstacles.

July 2000

I DIDN'T GET the degree! I was permanently expelled from the college without the college giving any reason for doing so. No lawyer would help me sue because I couldn't afford to pay them.

My and Five Others' Views
on the Primary Purposes of Education

WHEN I THINK about what the primary purposes of education (schooling, Kindergarten through 12th Grade) are, I think of what they often seem to me to be in contrast to what I think, feel, and believe, respectively, they should be. The primary purposes of education seem to be to babysit, and to inculcate the majority's acceptable social mores of American society. The latter consist of obedience to authority (first and foremost) and thereby to allow others to control one's destiny instead of oneself controlling one's own destiny. Further, schools expect people to follow convention and conventional wisdom in all its forms. It seems that schooling does not even succeed with these (unworthy) purposes.

What I think should be the purposes of education (and schooling) are to allow students to learn self-direction in most things, and so to learn to know when to question authority, rather than simply obeying in all or most things without question. To thereby gain the ability to truly think for themselves apart from what society might say is "right" and "good," even perhaps to learn to better understand what people generally consider "wrong" and/or "bad" both within themselves and the world around them. For, the "wrong" and "bad," if we tell the truth about ourselves, are ineradicable parts of each and all of us, as well as the "good" and "right," which we discover very early on, to our individual and collective dismay. To then help students discern if these designations of "right" and "good," "wrong," and "bad" are realties in and of themselves, applicable in some situations, but not others, or outright fallacies.

For instance, I am taking another class at Empire State College called "Thinking about Race, Gender and Class." The first premise one of the textbooks presents is the notion that there is no such reality in any physical sense of separate races among humans at all. I am open-minded in the extreme, and I found this shocking. So, how must others who are much more circumspect and conventional in their thinking react to such scientific evidence?

Most likely, they will do what I did at first, and dispute this with vigor and tenacity (and even much heat!) Unlike me, however, I get the impression that because of a majority's lack of schooling (and life education) in how to actually think logically and systematically, and how to revise deeply (and dearly!) held opinions when they receive new evidence to the contrary, they will not change their opinions to conform to the new information they got.

Most probably won't even understand such statements (as I, at first, didn't until I read further and thought more about them). Finally, the majority of people in whatever social context would not encourage such thought processes. Such thought processes make people too difficult to get along with, disturb the peace of mind of those who were at ease with the old (often mistaken) lines of reasoning, and make for much discomfort, both for the original thinker and her/his interlocutor.

Another example of the last sentence in the previous paragraph is the notion of mental illness that the majority of persons hold in America, and perhaps all over the world, for all I know. There are still psychological professionals (some with impeccable credentials and much scientific evidence to back them up) who argue that such concepts as schizophrenia, bi-polar "disease," and other diagnoses found in the Diagnostic and Statistical Manual that psychological professionals of all stripes use to determine whether people are "mentally ill," are mere social constructs, and like the social construct of race, have no physical or other reality than social. Every single person I have ever asked about the reality of so-called mental illness has stridently affirmed its reality outside of people believing it to be real!

I would now like to move yet further into the social sphere through the topic of this paper and say that I was surprised at the viewpoints of my interviewees. Most are people I have been associating with for years, although rather loosely in two cases, and only for one year in one case. I thought I knew what to expect from these individuals in response to the question, "What do you think, feel, believe, are the primary purposes of education?"

With the consensus of thought that I perceive that our society encourages, whether covertly, overtly, intentionally, or unintentionally, I was sure that I would get the same high-minded response from all my interlocutors. I thought that they would all say something to the effect that the primary purposes of education are to teach people how to think for themselves. In fact only one of my interviewees said this. He is a traditional Episcopal Minister at the Church which owns the apartment building I live in. He has a 9-year-old daughter who attends a private "religious" school, as he himself characterized it. In addition to believing that schools should teach people how to think for themselves, he agreed that they don't often achieve that goal.

Another thing that surprised me in my interviewees' responses, was their willingness to respond at all. No one demurred from responding by saying that s/he didn't have an opinion. Also, all responses, even of a retired public elementary school principal, with at least one grown daughter of her own, struck me as vague. The retired principal stated that she felt that the primary purposes of education are to help people live better in all aspects of life, e.g., morally, financially, and socially. I found this vague because, taking on just the departments of life she mentioned, one could easily debate what "better" means in those contexts.

For instance, is morally better, "blowing the whistle" on something you know to be detrimental that people you have a vested interest with are doing, e.g., the company you work for, your government, other authorities, people you feel emotionally close to and/or beholden to, responsible for, etc. even though you could lose a great deal that you value very highly in the bargain? Does it mean following one's own conscience in the way of the early Christians or blacks during the Civil Rights Movement, when you're in a despised minority and know that you could lose your very life for doing so?

Does living "better" financially mean helping others less fortunate with whatever amount of money one has, or does it mean making as much money as one can and then doing philanthropical things with it, if at all? How about socially? Does it mean moving only in "better" social circles? What/who do they consist of? Do they consist of people with money, "culture" (whose culture?), high moral standards (which brings us back to our original question) or what? All these things, my retired elementary school principal did not elucidate upon. I think she felt that all "right thinking (feeling, believing)" people would know what she meant, and that common sense would dictate the specifics. However, I'm not so sure about that, as I hope I have made plain in all of the above.

Two other surprising interviewees were a blue (pink) collar school worker and a white collar professional who is the manager of my apartment building. Although there were shades of difference in their responses, I think their responses were alike. Their responses were also alike in their being utilitarian in their approaches, much like my retired elementary school principal's was, rather than schooling for schooling's sake.

The pink collar school worker stated that the primary purposes of education are to impart knowledge (again, rather vague, i.e., what/which knowledge?) and so that one can pursue one's chosen profession. I tried to make my interviewees understand that we were talking about schooling of children from Kindergarten through 12th grade. However, they did not revise their opinions once they understood this.

The white collar professional manager of my apartment building stated something to the effect that the primary purpose of education is to afford greater social and financial opportunities. Again, this is rather vague. Does education afford a "better," e.g., more stable, fruitful, and fulfilling marriage (it hasn't for me!), "better," e.g., more loyal, trustworthy, helpful, friends and associates, etc.?

Finally, I asked a successful entrepreneur associate of mine, who has four children, what he thought the primary purposes of education are. He seconded me, only in the negative, or present, primary purposes. He said that he believed that the present primary purposes of education are to teach obedience, and how to be a follower instead of a leader, and to learn to let others control one rather than controlling one's own destiny.

I would say that, in the main, from my interviewees' responses, many people have never really thought very deeply about the philosophical aspects of schooling, even the retired elementary school principal, but take as their own, the conventional wisdom about schooling that our society would have us believe. I was surprised at the Episcopal Minister's thought that the primary purpose of education is to teach people to think for themselves because, I don't think, feel, or believe that Christianity, teaches people to think; rather, it teaches people to believe blindly.

As for the entrepreneur, who agreed with me (although in the negative), we are both very strong-willed people who have our own thoughts on how to do things and have had our share of clashes in the past. However, we do agree on many things and have kept a friendly demeanor toward each other over many years, in spite of our clashes. So, I was not surprised to hear him agreeing with me.

In summary, I will say that from my interviewees, it seems that two possible reasons for the vagueness of their answers are: 1) many people (no matter how well schooled) do not think very deeply about education (or much of anything else, for that matter), mainly, I believe, because society does not encourage them to; or 2) my interviewees simply did not express themselves clearly under the duress of my spontaneous question. The white collar professional manager of my building did originally say that she would like to give me her answer the next day, but emphatically stuck with her original position after I asked her near the end of our conversation if she would like to respond the next day.

As Socrates discovered in ancient Athens, at the cost of his life, most people do not question their assumptions and are violently opposed to anyone asking them to. This Socrates life proved all that long time ago, and mine proves today!

September 2001

My Informed Opinions
On Higher Education

UNFORTUNATELY, IT SEEMS that the "3 'Rs,'" Reading, 'Riting, and 'Rithmetic, which are the basics that are necessary for a decent education, go so fundamentally lacking at all levels of education, and most surprisingly so, at the level of higher education. Again, unfortunately, most of the people in my milieu lack them to a considerable degree regardless of the level of their education. I have many examples of this, of which I will cite a few here.

In 1991, I started a home word processing service. Over one Fall semester, approximately September to January, I typed course papers for approximately six or seven college students, between the ages of late teens to 70, from freshman in college to Ivy League Graduate School, i.e., Columbia Graduate School of Social Work. All of these, by the way, thought that because I was a mere typist (correcting their atrocious grammar, spelling, and punctuation, as well as their incorrect facts, for pay), who inglamorously worked at home in her bathrobe at times, and they were in the rarefied atmosphere of higher academia, they were by far more intelligent than I was, knew more than I did, and, I'm sure, felt they were morally superior to me (insofar as they thought at all!), from the first of them to the last of them!

In any case, not one of them, as I have hinted above, could read well or write well; "Ms. Columbia Graduate School of Social Work" went on to earn her degree, I lamentably add, and particularly, could not write in complete sentences! The 70-year-old told me, by way of apology, that he used to be very good at English, but over the years, in spite of his assiduous reading and studying, he'd lost "the knack," so to speak, for using it correctly (I can't tell you how many times I have heard this particular lament, and if it is true [which I doubt], I hope it never happens to me!)

Yet another student was a political science major whose native language was not English. His school papers were relatively good (but were "nothing to write home about," as the saying goes, in my opinion), but he later wrote a novel, which he paid to have published, the language of which was so stilted and boring as to be almost unintelligible! I was dumbfounded by the impossibly poor quality of his book because I had picked him out as the only one who had even a passable grasp of the English Language although it was not his *lingua franca*! To top this off, most of these students were very reluctant to pay the comparatively inexpensive price I was charging to make them look like they actually knew what they were talking about!

So, as a practical experiment, although very small, 100% of these students of all ages, all grade levels, and all types of schools and backgrounds, were lacking in the most basic reading and writing skills. (I wouldn't want to begin to see their arithmetic skills; although I know one woman who states that she hates to read [to the point that she hasn't read a three-page letter I sent to her over two weeks ago] but is astute at geometry, trigonometry, and algebra! I find this hard to believe, as I do most of what she says.) This is truly appalling!

With the depth of some of the emotions I have at almost any time I can think of, I am often, even with my extreme ability to articulate what is on my mind, at a loss to find words in which to couch those feelings. How then can these people communicate the agonies and ecstasies of existence without proper communication skills except in the most simple-minded ways imaginable, in spite of their college degrees? How can they connect with others through language (meaning, how much can they understand, as well as articulate what they understand) without a rudimentary and clear understanding of how to manipulate, at the very least, their native language? How can they even think clearly? I have found the unfortunate answer to all those questions to be: they can't!

Another problem I find from this lack of ability to use the English Language proficiently in all walks of life around me, is that people cannot easily learn how to pronounce unfamiliar words, for they don't have the ability to "sound them out," or use what is known as "phonics." Almost invariably, when I see someone confronted with a word s/he doesn't know, especially if it is latinate, or a complicated medical term (same thing), etc., s/he simply cannot pronounce it! S/he just can't wrap her/his tongue around those polysyllables.

Because I am not an educator, and because I know how to "do" English, but would find myself hard-pressed to teach anyone who doesn't know how to "do" it, to "do" it, I do not know what the solutions to this problem are. (I have found Diana Hacker's *A Writer's Reference* invaluable in my own studies.) I also have had the same twelve to thirteen years of basic education that everyone else in this country gets (although I started out in another land, the Bahamas, from which, when I first came to America at the age of seven, the school I attended put me in the "slowest" class, because, I believe, Americans [in their infinite arrogance] think that every other country is more backward than them, especially in education, whether that is true or not! Most teachers are [or used to be] pretty smart, even wise, and mine quickly realized their mistake with me). I don't see how anyone can go through twelve to thirteen years of schooling, college notwithstanding, and not know how to read, write, multiply, divide, add, and subtract! That is a reality for so many people in this country that I find it hard to wrap my mind around it, as it were; if I'm not mistaken, one of the last despised bastions of communism (beside China), Cuba, has an almost perfect literacy rate! What does that say about America? Not much that's good, I'd venture!

Almost Every aspect of life suffers from lack of these skills. For instance, one can't even have a decent conversation without getting sidetracked, going into digressions from the subject at hand (to the point where everyone concerned can no longer discern what the subject ever was to begin with), and getting into arguments because people don't understand the meanings of the words one is using, etc. All this comes from woolly thinking, which so many people are guilty of. This is because no one ever taught them how to think, and because these people conspired in "dumbing themselves down," as the saying is, by buying into what the people who taught them not to think tell them to think, about themselves and their world. I learned long ago that being too scholarly, learned, and independent of mind is not socially acceptable among the masses in this country, lip service to the contrary notwithstanding! It's like having a communicable disease most of the time because of the general low level of people in this country, in that area; people avoid one like the plague!

An article in the New York Times in 1993 noted another example of the trend of college-educated people not truly being educated, even on a minimum level, such as in the "3 'Rs'." It discussed the findings of a report sponsored by four foundations. Witness: "It [the report] cites as evidence the National Adult Literacy Survey, which found *large numbers of college graduates lacking basic reading, writing and computation skills*" (emphasis mine) ("Report" A46). And, "The report asserts that American universities certify for graduation too many students who cannot read and write very well, too many whose intellectual depth and breadth are unimpressive, and too many whose skills are inadequate in the face of the demands of contemporary life'" (qtd. in "Report" A46).

This was in 1993. However, the situation does not seem to be improving and without those basic skills, everything else falls by the wayside. Without these basic skills, one might be able to adequately get along, with or without a so- called college education, but one will never be able to fulfill the promise of much of one's inherent potential, which can be hard enough to do with these skills. I don't think that institutions of higher learning are the place to teach these skills, but should be places for broadening one's mastery of this and other knowledge. However, these institutions cannot do the latter unless, somehow, someone can inculcate those basic skills before then somewhere along the line in the educational process; if not, as I have found, over and over again, higher education can be nothing more than a bad joke!

May 2000

Thinkfest 2004

It is Thanksgiving Day, and as I sit here waiting for my turkey to finish cooking (or is it my getting my "goose cooked" with what I'm about to say?), I'm reading a book called, The Matrix and Philosophy, which contains essays in which their authors discuss the philosophical and religious ramifications of the movie, "The Matrix." In the introduction, the editor names some philosophers and then says that some of the questions their ideas (philosophies) help us to address in our lives are: "What can I know?" "What is freedom and do we have it?" "What should I do?" "What may I hope?"[1] I would like to address these questions here, and I would like to ask some more questions for what I hope will be a "Thinkfest," or festival of deep thinking.

For most people, it seems, I find that they believe they have answered most questions on how to conduct themselves (or at least how others should conduct themselves!), etc., and the answers are usually static ones handed down pre-made by tradition and common sense, especially when these people are confronted by the startling, even down-right shocking, or unusual.

For instance, the question, "What can I know?" usually amounts to what everyone thinks or believes they know to be true. However, the closest definition I have gotten as to what truth is is the following, "Truth is what is so about something, the reality of the matter, as distinguished from what people wish were so, believe to be so, or assert to be so. . .people do not create truth. . .Does the truth ever change? No. . .The truth will not be changed by our knowledge or our ignorance. . .It is obvious that situations in which we believe we know but really don't know pose an obstacle to effective thinking. Why should anyone go to the trouble to investigate a matter or listen to opposing testimony if one believes one knows already?"[2]

To really incite deep thinking (learning), which I understand one can do like inciting a riot[3], I ask, do we "know" that men landed on the Moon? How do we know? Can we "know" that? I have a video tape of a TV show, and a book review, both of which purport that men did not land upon the lunar surface.[4,5]

When I have even brought this possibility up to people, they have become stunned and couldn't even begin to think how this could not have happened as NASA professed it did. It's like questioning whether Jesus was a god, or any better or different than anyone can be! The conversation usually comes to an upbrupt halt when I further explain to these people that the only thing absolutely certain about their belief in this matter, like most of their beliefs, is that they believe it (them), notwithstanding, that they believe these things in common with a great many people. I've offered to show the video to one man who refused to view it. Another man viewed the video and started calling upon God to save him (us) from the devil (another unfortunately pat response). This response, seemingly drawn up from the depths, at least is in line with the compelling nature of the facts the video presented against the proposition that men landed on the Moon. Such facts, should we give them the slightest credence in line with the evidence that supports them, may teach us not to be so smugly sure about what everyone "knows" and how they have come to "know" it, or at least think they know it.

Another question to which most give very little thought, which I have discussed in the "Letters to the Editor" column of Horoscope[6] previously is, "Is there such a thing as mental illness?" Does behavior that seems crazy or unconventional justify us in saying that someone is "mentally ill?" What does the term "mental illness" really mean, anyway?

Most people never even give these questions a second thought, nor do they look at scientific evidence that very astutely clarifies the reality of what we mean when we use the term "mental illness" (even if they could understand what they are seeing!) One reason that this is true is that most people have never been accused of having "mental illness," which accusation can often lead to incarceration without a trial and without having been charged with any crime, and automatic stigmatization of the "culprit" for the rest of her/his life. Our social institutions have decided what the meanings of the term "mental illness" are and you'd better agree and behave accordingly or you could lose your liberty and a whole lot else besides, as I have stated above.

That brings us to the question, "What is freedom and do we have it?" I have found throughout my lifetime, as did Socrates in ancient Athens, literally at the cost of his life, that we are free to agree with what everyone else in our social milieu thinks, feels, and believes, or to suffer endlessly, in all kinds of ways, for not doing so. It is the rare person who does not suffer these agonies endlessly at the hands of her/his compatriots for so deviating from the status quo, as history has shown down through the ages, and as is still the case.

In witness of this I offer the following excerpt from Alexis de Tocqueville's book, *Democracy in America*, which is one of the most eloquent descriptions of the above-mentioned fate that I have read:

"In America the majority has enclosed thought within a formidable fence. A writer [or heretic, in my case who boldly and courageously opposes these boundaries, calls a lie a lie and speaks the truth as I see it] is free inside that area, but woe to the man who goes beyond it. Not that he stands in fear of an auto-da-fe [burning at the stake], but he must face all kinds of unpleasantness and everyday persecution. A career in politics is closed to him, for he has offended the only power that holds the keys. He is denied everything, including renown. Before he goes into print, he believes he has supporters; but he feels that he has them no more once he stands revealed to all, for those who condemn him express their views loudly, while those who think as he does, but without his courage, retreat into silence as if ashamed of having told the truth.

"Formerly tyranny used the clumsy weapons of chains and hangmen; nowadays even despotism, though it seemed to have nothing more to learn, has been perfected by civilization. Princes made violence a physical thing, but our contemporary democratic republics have turned it into something as intellectual as the human will it is intended to constrain. Under the absolute government of a single man, despotism, to reach the soul, clumsily struck at the body, and the soul escaping from such blows, rose gloriously above it; but in democratic republics that is not at all how tyranny behaves; it leaves the body alone and goes straight for the soul. The master no longer says: 'Think like me or you die.' He does say: 'You are free not to think as I do; you can keep your life and property and all; but from this day you are a stranger among us. You can keep your privileges in the township, but they will be useless to you, for if you solicit your fellow citizens' votes, they will not give them to you, and if you only ask for their esteem, they will make excuses for refusing that. You will remain among men, but you will lose your rights to count as one. When you approach your fellows, they will shun you as an impure being, and even those who believe in your innocence will abandon you too, lest they in turn be shunned. Go in peace, I have given you your life, but it is a life worse than death.'

"Absolute monarchies brought despotism into dishonor; we must beware lest democratic republics rehabilitate it, and that while they make it more oppressive toward some, they do not rid it of its detestable and degrading character in the eyes of the greatest number.

"In the proudest nations of the Old World works were published which faithfully portrayed the vices and absurdities of contemporaries; La Bruyere lived in Louis XIV's palace while he wrote his chapter on the great, and Moliere criticized the court in plays acted out before the courtiers. But the power which dominates the United States does not understand being mocked like that. The least reproach offends it, and the slightest sting of truth turns it fierce; and one must praise everything, from the turn of its phrases to its most robust virtues. No writer, no matter how famous, can escape from this obligation to sprinkle incense over his fellow citizens. Hence the majority lives in a state of perpetual self-adoration; only strangers or experience may be able to bring certain truths to the Americans' attention.

"We need seek no other reason for the absence of great writers in America so far; literary genius cannot exist without freedom of the spirit, and there is no freedom of the spirit in America.

"In Spain the Inquisition was never able to prevent the circulation of books contrary to the majority religion. The American majority's sway extends further and has rid itself even of the thought of publishing such books. One finds unbelievers in America, but unbelief has, so to say, no organ.

"One finds governments striving to protect mores by condemning the authors of licentious books. No one in the United States is condemned for works of that sort, but no one is tempted to write them. Not that all the citizens are chaste in their mores, but those of the majority are regular.

"In this, no doubt, power is well used, but my point is the nature of the power in itself. This irresistible power is a continuous fact and its good use only an accident. . .The influence of what I have been talking about is as yet only weakly felt in political society, but its ill effects on the national character are already apparent. I think that the rareness now of outstanding men on the political scene is due to the ever-increasing despotism of the American majority [this in the early 1800's!] When the Revolution broke out, a crowd of them appeared; at that time public opinion gave direction to men's wills but did not tyrannize over them. The famous men of that time, while they freely took part in the intellectual movement of the age, had a greatness all their own; their renown brought honor to the nation, not vice versa. . .[T]here is a great difference between doing something of which you do not approve and pretending to approve of what you are doing; the first is the part of a weak man, but the second fits only the manners of a valet."[7]

"What should I do?" is another quite daunting question, partially stemming from both the first and second questions I posed here. If we look closely, we can see, envision, that all the questions we are considering here influence each other. I would like to give what I believe to be an excellent example of an answer to the question, "What should I do?" or rather "What shouldn't I do?" (a "homey" example, as its author describes it), which illustrates how we might answer this question under astrological duress, namely prolonged outer planet transits; which duress we can all, I'm sure, attest to having been under at one time or another:

"One day we get angry with our neighbor, and have an almost irresistible impulse to heave a rock over the fence through his window, get him out in the yard, and beat him up. Custom, however, has taught us that this is not the way civilized people behave; we know that we should not act in heat or anger or momentary rage; so when we get this savage rage, something automatically says no, and we refrain. We'll at least think it over. We bide our time. Three months later, we get the same urge all over again. By this time, we have been unconsciously whipping ourselves into a frenzy of righteous wrath over our neighbor. His kids trample the flowers. His wife doesn't cover the garbage pail. His dog is a nuisance, we don't like his politics, and he doesn't say hello on the bus. So, when we get the fighting urge later, we are convinced that we have been patient, and have waited. So, with the comforting thought that we have turned it over in our mind, we act. The result is precisely the same as if we had heaved the rock the first time we felt like it."[8]

As for the final question, "What may I hope," I would like to say with Judi Thomases[9], and many other astrologers, that astrologically speaking, one can safely look to one's natal Jupiter and one's North Node positions to best determine the answers to that question. However, as one final note, I will add that what one may hope is bounded by influences which I believe we cannot fully know unless we peek (peak?) into the very source of what powers our lives. Very few of us get to do this while we live.

I have hoped for and dared things in my life that still have not panned out, and I have dared some things, but not hoped for success and yet have achieved it. My life remains achingly difficult because of all of the above and for other reasons I can't sufficiently fathom. However, I continue to hope and to trust that although I am stepping out into my future (literally!) without a notion of what it will bring me, I am similar in this regard to, though not exactly like, a caterpillar in its cocoon, going through her transformation, trusting, without consciously knowing that in the end of my journey, I will arise as a butterfly, with lovely gossamer wings that will allow me to soar to any and all heights of which my spirit is capable. This is nothing more than the lesson of faith. May you in the end find the courage to do the same!

Notes:

1. William Irwin, ed., *The Matrix and Philosophy*, (Peru: Carus Publishing, 2002), 2.
2. Vincent Ryan Ruggiero, *The Art of Thinking A Guide to Critical and Creative Thought*, 5th ed., (New York: Addison Wesley Longman, Inc., 1998), 23-25.
3. Audre Lorde, *Sister Outsider*, (Trumansburg: Crossing Press, 1984), 98.
4. Conspiracy Theory: Did We Land on the Moon? Fox Channel, New York, 21 Mar. 2001.
5. Thomas J. Brown, review and commentary of NASA Mooned America, by Rene, *Borderlands Journal*, 4th Qtr. (1995): 52-56.
6. Donna Lee, letter, *Horoscope*, October (2002): 6.
7. Alexis de Tocqueville, *Democracy in America*, (New York: Alfred A. Knopf, 1945), 264-266.
8. Grant Lewi, *Astrology for the Millions*, (New York: Bantam Books, 1977), 347.
9. Judi Thomases, "Redesign Your Life in 2005! A 10-Step Plan for Taking Charge and Creating Change," *Horoscope*, January (2005): 18-23.

Human Composition and Love

Am I, are all of us, reducible to a mere conglomeration of neurotic, even psychotic, tendencies or adaptations or maladaptations to life and the world as it is, even when trying to change it, change ourselves? Or is there something more?

I feel like one day there was a rent made in the fabric of my illusions. I peered through it and once having glimpsed what lay behind, beyond it, I was never able to look at those illusions the same way again. I am thus haunted by a sense of the futility of all human endeavor no matter how grand (but we feel we must do something!) except perhaps as we better learn to love one another. It seems that that is the only truly worthwhile endeavor, which in its composition includes knowledge, understanding--wisdom, even--and is a woman like me.

This, however--loving--seems to be the one thing we feel we only have a certain amount of in our hearts to go round, when, truly, the heart can absolutely overflow with love and the joy attendant to it. Like, and liking, of course is quite another story and seems to satisfy the urge for comfort rather than the capacity for ecstasy and revelation, as well as the depths of feeling and darkness that the ability to love deeply and widely provides. Most people, cowards that they are, seek for the seemingly more benevolent, uncomplicated, liking of their fellows in general, over loving them. I seek it too, for the comfort it can provide me, has provided me in the past. However, the more complicated forces of "agape" and "eros" relate me absolutely to my fellows in the tangles of enmity, as well as in pleasurable "friendship," binds me to them in rage, as well as in the vision of the potential I see of what it may come to mean to be human rather than what we think it means already (as though humanity were not as much becoming what it will be as being what it is). For loving is all this, whereas liking is a blander sort of relationship, if it is that at all, and does not bind so tightly nor lay open to being so utterly torn asunder both inwardly and outwardly, does not encompass the magnitude of risk and vulnerability and therefore does not deliver the fuller rewards.

No, I think I will stick to loving while trying to discover if I am capable of simply liking or disliking people again, rather than always only loving the spark of divinity in them, whether visible or not, and hating the weaknesses that make them base.

October 1991

About the Author

DONNA LEE IS interested in all literary and scholarly pursuits. In 2004, she started seriously writing short stories from a first sentence given to her by interested parties, in the tradition of the great Danish storyteller, Isak Dinesen, with rave reviews from most of the parties in question. If you're interested, please see below on how to submit your sentence to her. The extremely prestigious astrology journal, The Mountain Astrologer, published one of her articles, called "Saturn and the Shadow," in their Feb./Mar. 2005 issue. She has also contributed letters, fillers, and an article called "Jung's Personality Types and Astrology," this latter published in the May 2005 issue, to Dell Horoscope magazine. She will be publishing the above-mentioned short stories in the back of her upcoming book, Inquiry Journal Compilation, Volume I, a book of pithy, thought-provoking and inspiringly quotable quotes! Some specific scholarly pursuits she's especially interested in are Greek mythology, ancient Greek history, dream analysis, the lost continent of Atlantis, reincarnation, millennial prophecies, numerology, the psychological theories of Carl Jung, and astrology, all of which she's been studying mainly as an autodidact (self-taught person) for over 25 years. The C. G. Jung Institute in Zurich, Switzerland, gave her permission to paraphrase some of Jung's basic thought in five-minute voice recordings for a metaphysical 900 number hotline she instituted with a partner, Tony Pica, in 1994, and again, with a New York State grant, in 1995. This hotline is no longer extant. She is single and lives in Jamaica, New York. Contact her at her e-mail at mysticsource@hotmail.com. Write the word SENTENCE, in all capital letters, in the subject area of your e-mails.